CW00501330

# To Coventry by Sun

# To Coventry by Sun

*Poems from Twin Cities*

Nine
Arches
Press

**To Coventry by Sun**
***Poems from Twin Cities***

ISBN: 978-1-913437-33-6
Copyright © the individual authors and artists.

All rights reserved. No part of this work may be reproduced, stored or transmitted in any form or by any means, graphic, electronic, recorded or mechanical, without the prior written permission of the publisher.

The individual authors and artists have asserted their right under Section 77 of the Copyright, Designs and Patents Act 1988 to be identified as the authors of their work.

First published September 2021 by:

**Nine Arches Press**
Unit 14, Sir Frank Whittle Business Centre,
Great Central Way, Rugby.
CV21 3XH
United Kingdom

www.ninearchespress.com

Printed in the United Kingdom by:
Imprint Digital

Nine Arches Press is supported using public funding by Arts Council England.

Supported using public funding by
ARTS COUNCIL
ENGLAND

# CONTENTS

# FOREWORD

Coventry was the first city in the world to formally 'twin' itself with another when it twinned with Volgograd (then Stalingrad) in Russia in the midst of the Second World War in 1944. This extraordinary act of civic, international friendship made in dark and frightening times, not only withstood the decades of Cold War that followed, but was only the beginning of Coventry's unique twin-city story.

Throughout the twentieth century, Coventry continued to twin with other cities, making connection and friendship with a further twenty-five cities around the world. Some of these civic twinnings, with cities like Dresden, Kiel, Warsaw and Lidice, acknowledged connection through the traumatic experiences of war, with Coventry's post-war vision of peace and reconciliation in mind. Twin cities like Kingston and Cork acknowledge a connection through migration, as new citizens of Coventry, some of whom arrived as part of the Windrush generation from the Caribbean, or (like my own grandparents) from Ireland, and came to make the city their home. Other twinnings acknowledge fellowship with cities and towns of Coventry in the United States, or cement the deep ties that still remain with continental European cities such as Bologna, St Etienne and Graz.

Its legacy continues today – not least in the form of Coventry and Cork's Twin City Poetry exchange, initiated by poet Paul Casey in 2008, host and organiser of Cork's legendary Ó Bhéal live poetry series, and has continued since with support from writers in Coventry including Antony Owen, Adam Steiner and Raef Boylan. Each year, two poets from each city have travelled to experience life and poetry in each other's cities. Having been fortunate enough to have been 'exchanged' as a twin city poet (in 2018 with Peter Raynard) I've experienced for myself how enjoyable and valuable this exchange is – not least in celebrating a commonality through poetry with each other, whichever city we call our home.

The Twin Cities of Friendship postcard project, as a part of BBC Contains Strong Language festival of poetry (and part of Coventry's City of Culture 2021 year of events), set out to explore the further legacy of Coventry's 77-year project of civic, international friendship by commissioning a total of 20 poets – ten from Coventry and the local region (or with long connections to the city) and ten from a selection of Coventry's Twin Cities around the world.

Throughout the summer of 2021, postcards, designed by Coventry artists, which you can see here in this anthology, criss-crossed the globe, bearing messages and questions – *What is the weather like where you are? Who are your city's notable figures? What are your favourite buildings or places?* Finally, we asked each poet to write a poem that resulted from this exchange and to share these poems as an act of friendship with each other and their cities.

Having just been through the long pandemic winter of 2020-21 and the experiences of lockdown and isolation, this was also a vital project of reconnection – of looking outward from our windows, homes and familiar streets and imagining life beyond amber and red lists, quarantine and travel restrictions. What does it mean, after a time of disconnection and isolation during the global pandemic, to make contact with writers around the world and exchange poems and postcards – to be sent *to* and to be sent *from* Coventry?

It's been fascinating reading the conversations on postcards and the poems that have resulted. Aside from admiring the stamps, postmarks and array of scenic views from other cities, observing how a line or two in biro has sparked and spiralled between writers – giving space and voice to new poems – has been a real pleasure. As David Morley writes in his poem in response to Sarah Rehm in Dresden: "Your lines spin twinned between voices of this ghazal / and our voices twine around its lines."

Each poet responded to each other with generosity, creativity and openness; some imagined cities they had not visited and could not presently travel to, but conjured them to mind through their exchanges. Poet and translator Dušica Karaić from Belgrade, Serbia, felt moved by the exchanges between Olga Dermott-Bond and Mihajlo Žilović and responded by writing the wonderful poem 'Golden Light' which opens this anthology. Others looked to the past and present, for historic figures and unique stories, or to the daily life, routines and habits of their home cities.

These threads of connection, in an uncertain world seem ever more important, as do the international bonds of friendship that Coventry and its twenty-six twin cities established over several decades since 1944. Long may we continue to look out from our windows and think beyond borders, and long may we extend a words of fellowship in scribbled notes on postcards as they cross between nations, poets and pen-friends.

I will leave you with these powerful lines from poet Tanya Shirley, writing from Kingston, Jamaica:

> Instead, two poets make worlds
> out of words, twining our desire for that which washes
> away, an undercurrent of all we cannot say
> on this page so small, so square, so public.

**Jane Commane.**

Editor, Nine Arches Press
September 2021

DUŠICA KARAIĆ

# Golden light

Some other day and some other time I'll be in Coventry.
Looking. Feeling. Tasting.

Taking in all the beauty there is to take.
Walking down the streets – all in stone!

Cathedrals in Goth style.
Their pointy tops so tall, they reach deeper, into my chest.

At night everything enlightens – gold that lines my heart,
warm golden light.

Suddenly I feel like I've been here before.
I've seen these buildings and windows.

But where? In frames, in pictures, on the edge of my dreams?
On postcards?

– That must be it! – I shout.
A woman with a baby looks at me strangely and walks away.

On postcards I've seen it, long ago, that one summer.
The river Sowe under the ink.

Lady Godiva riding a horse between the lines.
And my heart was protesting too.

I wanted to fly there,
I wanted to leave the border formed of paper and dust.

To feel the golden light of Coventry.

Image: Mary Courtney – 'To Coventry by Sun'

TO COVENTRY
BY SUN
MOON CRESCENT
The Star Motor Cycle
MARS
Villiers 269cc
J.A.P. 293cc
J.A.P. 350cc
Blackburn 350cc
Blackburn SPORTS
ECLIPSE
SUNNYSIDE CLOSE
3009 COVENTRY
URBAN ASTRONAUT

БЕОГРАД, Нови Двор
BELGRADE. Le nouveau palais royal
THE ARDS PENINSULA

# BELGRADE

**Beograd / Београд**
**Serbia**

*Twinned in 1957*

**44°49′N 20°28′E**
**1,127 miles from Coventry**

MIHAJLO ŽILOVIĆ

OLGA DERMOTT-BOND

MIHAJLO ŽILOVIĆ

## Bermingem, pa Koventri, Beograd

Bermingem, pa Koventri, Beograd,
Isto prvo slovo,
bogatstvo napisanih reči, čestitke, sve novo!

Ne sećam se dana,
da sam nekom pis'o,
i da meni neko piše,
rukopise, razglednice.

Kultura je druga,
stil života isto,
jedino nas veže,
poezija, umetnost, bajnost, i sva druga sličnost.

Saznao sam mnogo, dosta,
Olga divno o svom gradu piše,
čekajuci nestrpljivo napisane razglednice.

I ja sam joj puno rek'o,
o Moskvi, Dvoru, pismu,
Desanci, Branku i mnogim sličnim – stvarima ćirilicnim.

Sve ću ovo zaokružiti jednom mišlju divnom,
volimo Vas gde god da ste,
neka vlada sloga ljubav i večiti mir!

## Birmingham, Coventry and Belgrade

Birmingham, Coventry and Belgrade
First letter is the same
The beauty of written words, postcards,
Everything in unfamiliar frame

Hardly I remember those days
when I used to write to someone
And that one to reply in his ways,
handwritings, letters and postcards

The culture is different
and the way of life
But what bounds us –
Poetry, artistry
and speaking lyrically

Plenty have I learned,
Olga writes of her city beautifully,
Waiting impatiently,
for the postcards to arrive

And I also told her a lot,
Of Moscow hotel, the Old Palace,
Desanka, Branko and the others well depict – in Cyrillic script

This I will finish
with one lovely thought –
Wherever you go and stay, all of you we love in the same way!

**Translated by Dušica Karaić**

OLGA DERMOTT-BOND

# To reach you

*Azbuka (азбука)*

I study the stamps, printed in Cyrillic script
Д **И Љ**. Of course. Not only a different language
but each word born from intricate letters,
mirror images of my own. I begin to scrutinise
*your* ***азбука;*** such delicate ladders, curlicues,
that have been posted through my front door.

*Mihajlo*

My house is suddenly full of yellow flowers
when you write to me, a little thrill as I hold
your thought in my hands – this frail fortress
of cardboard and ink we are building, two sides
of one story. *Mihajlo.* Your name means
archangel and I kneel at these flimsy visitations.

***the Mosvka hotel***

You tell me about the beauty of Belgrade
at night, send me a picture of floodlit bridges.
I imagine myself at the Mosvka hotel, sipping *Rakija*
beneath gilt ceilings, standing on the Kalemegdan
walls, finding you there, where the Danube
and Sova meet, two rivers kissing.

## *Journey*

I will go there one day, I decide. The perforated
edges of every day become a thrumming track: I trace
my route – *Coventry, Euston, St Pancras, Kings Cross,*
*Gare de Mulhouse, Basel, Lugano, Milano, Bologna,*
*Trieste, Belgrade.* Clean sheets, rocked to sleep
as the night train crumples borders, east and further east.

## *Landlocked*

I take my pen. The familiar ritual of my left side
a comfort, the right side for your address, copied
so carefully each time. Some mornings I am moss
half-buried amongst the grass of days, landlocked
and heart slower than stone, but to reach you with
six lines is to migrate towards some unvisited place.

## *Desanka*

You write to me about Desanka Maksimović
how her poetry speaks of a country of villagers.
Now, each postcard is a glittering pasture full
of her blue mountains, ravens, moons. I think of us
in our rooms, shrinking down our days to fit the lines,
read her work again; *as though slowly a door were opening –*

Image: Gurdip Junjuha – 'Solving the solution'

BOLOGNA
PER TUTTE LE ALTRE
BOLOGNA
La Dotta - La Grassa
TO COVENTRY
BY SUN

# BOLOGNA

**Bulåggna**

**Italy**

*Twinned in 1960*

44°29′38″N 11°20′34″E

801 miles from Coventry

*#NARRANDOBO*

LEONARDO BIANCONI, LEO MERATI,
and GIULIA QUADRELLI

AYSAR GHASSAN

## *#NARRANDOBO:* LEONARDO BIANCONI, LEO MERATI and GIULIA QUADRELLI

# 'Ricevi una cartolina da lontano...'

Ricevi una cartolina da lontano
ricevi la fotografia della stessa cartolina
da lontano.
Guardi la fotografia della cartolina
e scopri attorno la città vicina.
Una piccola pergola con le luci,
le corsie di un supermercato.
Molte volte
le buche delle lettere, tutte quante rosse,
ovunque, ma di un rosso diverso, ovunque.

Tutte le piazze sono in silenzio
ferragosto ha portato la gente al mare
non c'è nessuno per le strade
ed è così che sbucan fuori
come luci da luminarie
le buchette delle lettere.

Son rosse, timide e immobili
non si scostano dal portico
e paion voler aspettare
che passi una mano a lasciare
una lettera sul fondo del pianale.

Quando la pancia è piena
ruggiscono vocali
"Sara mi manchi"
"Saluta il babbo"
"Ciao da Bologna"
ed è bello accostarsi
per sentirle sussurrare.
Oggi, ad esempio, ha scritto
uno straniero, da lontano
oltre il mare
ha detto

Coventry, penso, è grigia e verde
fish and chips è una buona
tradizione il venerdì sera
il mio posto preferito è la mia casa –
no è il mio giardino.
Ho visto dei fiori sullo sfondo
della fotografia della cartolina
da lontano chissà se sono quelli del tuo giardino.

In una città che ho scoperto
è stata distrutta e poi ricostruita
come la mia città
all'angolo tra San Felice e Rivareno
all'angolo tra via Farini e Borgonuovo
all'angolo con Memorial Park
dove forse leggi una cartolina da lontano
che uno di noi tre ti ha spedito da qui
mentre mi viene questo pensiero

erano quattro anni che non compravo
un francobollo.

## 'You receive a postcard from afar...'

You receive a postcard from afar
you receive a photograph of the same postcard
from afar.
You look at the picture of the postcard and you
explore the nearby town.
A little pergola with lights,
the lanes of a supermarket.
Often letterboxes
are all red, everywhere, but a different red,
everywhere.

All the piazzas are silent
mid-August pushes people to the seaside
there's no one on the street
that's how they pop out
like bolts of lightning –
letter boxes.

They are red, timid, and motionless
they don't come out from the portico
and seem to be waiting
for a hand to come by and drop
a letter into their depths.

When their bellies are full
they rumble
"I miss you, Sara"
"Say Hi to father"
"Ciao from Bologna"
and it's lovely to get close
to hear their whispers.
Today, for example, wrote
a foreigner, from afar

beyond the sea
and said
Coventry, I think, is grey and green
fish and chips is good
a Friday evening tradition
my favourite place is my home –
no, it's my garden.
I saw some flowers in the background
of the photo on the postcard
from afar who knows if they're from your garden.

In a city that I discovered
was destroyed and then reconstructed
like my city
at the corner of San Felice and Rivareno
at the corner of via Farini and Borgonuovo
at the corner of Memorial Park
where maybe you read a postcard from afar
that one of us three sent from here
while I have this thought

it was four years that I hadn't bought
a postage stamp.

**Translated by Allison Grimaldi Donahue**

AYSAR GHASSAN

# The Postie Isn't Clutching Bills

*Hello!*
From my bay window I can see
a small car take up three parking spaces,
a little girl picking her nose and eating it.
The Crocosmias frown, my lawn needs edging.

There, you are an ice-cream, melting.
Here, it has cooled once more,
and I have been reconstituted,
slightly misshapen.

From my front garden I can hear
a seagull, lost, screeching expletives,
a van take a bite out of a kerb,
a tot mispronouncing 'cucumber',
families putting sniping aside in anticipation of dinner.

Your colours are long-cooked over a stove,
ours are a little grey, built post-war in a flourish,
sometimes dipped in curry sauce.
You bite into mortadella,
rounds of fat surrender to your tongue,
*I am ravenous!*
Why would you want to live elsewhere?

I am thinking about paprika crisps at the airport.
I type so much these days,
I am glad you can make out my writing.

**Image: Gayatri Pasricha– 'bare souls'**

TO COVENTRY
BLARNEY
CASTLE
FOTA
WILDLIFE PARK
THU

# CORK
## Corcaigh
## Ireland

*Twinned in 1958*

51°53′50″N 8°28′12″W
297 miles from Coventry

VICTORIA KENNEFICK

RAEF BOYLAN

VICTORIA KENNEFICK

## Portrait of Cork and Coventry as Twinned Poet Correspondents

Cork, ___

Dear ___, I can scarcely fit it all in
the confines of this small rectangular card,
there is so much to say, and these borders are sharp and
right-angled. I hate paper cuts. But I digress –
I make these hunched, cramped letters, shapes
with my pen to try to show you what I see –
the river Lee, rushing into town, running late for its date
with the ocean, frothing at the mouths of breweries.
Our difficult beloved sometimes threatens
to consume us in hungry, gushing gulps,
to flood us with its love and the memory
of its ancient meanders – pity, pity.
Best, ___

Coventry, ___

Dear ___, The Lee! Resist the push to channel its exuberance!
I see its curves in your tiny, awkward letters and I raise you
the Sherbourne that hides and sneaks in culverts beneath beautiful
Coventry. There is talk of its rising again and gurgling at The Burges.
Clear stream, a twin to yours, multiples to reflect our matching parks
and Cathedrals pushing the sky up and away, a collective canopy
as we share the cacophony of *C* and the deep
soulful pool of *O*. Cork, Coventry, O –
that's where we diverge.
Best, ___

Cork, ___

Dear, ___We keep it short – Cork, as in bottle,
stopping the jet on land we've clawed back. Coventry,
four extra letters stretched across the water (a *cove*, an *entry*),
we traversed in droves to escape the hunger, the horror –
what else could we do? Across the sea to you.
Look at us now – writing back and forth, cards instead of boats,
and the words, the words are the same – tiny, hunched things,
tiny, haunted things – a chain of peaks and dips ~ *batch, tripe,*
*God cake, Murphy's Stout* ~ Cork and Coventry. Alliterative friends/
CoCo forever!
Best now and always, ___

Coventry, ___

Dear___, CoCo! The curve of Pana, the timber frames of Spon Street, Fitzgerald Park, Lady Herbert's Garden – they intermingled in the words we squeezed around stamps for weeks. I see your blood. Paper cuts are brutal. Scars here too. See: The strata of our cities, built up, flattened, restored, part of each other now. The Lee that you write with such indentation becomes the Sherbourne through the card, and once more, the Lee. Both urge each other on, the impossible compulsion to flow into the sea. The reasons for streets, parks and cathedrals, watch how they become one when they're finally free.
Best eternally to you, friend, ___

**RAEF BOYLAN**

## *Be Rightly Proud*

*Cork is what I think of when I think 'city'*, she writes, and I
relate entirely – for me, Cov always collocates like that.

Fondness for *every slab and brick*, cobblestone, patch of grass
parcelled up in a few short paragraphs of rusty penmanship;

a gesture inspiring and fragile, like a shaky suspension bridge.
We reach out across the water, each extend a friendly hand,

offer little details embedded – portals to transport, to catch a glance
of the other's perspective – like gemstones smuggled from abroad.

To sample a red lemonade picnic in Fitzgerald's Park, or to tour
the English Market and buy tansy sauce with tripe and drisheen,

washed down with Beamish under a rainbow novelty,
umbrella-tented and pedestrianised; adapted to these al fresco times.

To drink in a street of Corkonian confidence, an anthem sublime
as the Bells of Shandon – accent *undulates, up and down,*

harmonised with the steep slopes and hillsides that abound
like nuggets of slang, evolving fast, to keep pace with the craic.

To stroll in the Lee's company: magnificent crease in the centre's map,
charging on, impervious to what is discussed and planned –

this river, sibling to the Sherbourne, too often reclaims the land
but, flooded with emotional support, resists a final resting place.

To pause beneath a nearby tree: the rasp as mallards mate
while toddlers laugh, mouths and hands smeared ice-cream sticky.

---

We share an aversion to *vandalising* the canvasses of our cities,
urban compulsion to seek out green spaces, any *oasis of calm.*

Like all twins, our cities have their differences, flaws and charms –
and we could blunder into competition, but instead choose

a dynamic where neither is deemed to win or lose,
since we celebrate them both with poetic interludes.

Image: Adele Mary Reed – 'K and I, 29th December, 2018'

BRICK SCHOOL
c.1825
COVENTRY HISTORICAL SOCIETY
Open First & Third Sundays May - Early Oct
1-4 PM

# COVENTRY, CT.

## USA

*Twinned in 1962*

41°47′04″N 72°20′20″W
3,271 miles from Coventry

SUSAN MACNEIL

EMILIE LAUREN JONES

SUSAN MACNEIL

## Stout Man, Untamed Woman

Words vibrated in the ether like fireworks.
Charmed remembrances quivered 3,500 miles 'across the pond,' so far away from the diminutive rural twin; the US namesake birthed in 1711. We extended an oath beyond country hills, dotted with farms and congeniality, to a citified Coventry with double-decker buses, the Beatles and a vernacular all its own. And so I brought my girlish cheerleading enthusiasm to our UK twin, honoring the past and renewing the present through the "City of Culture" recognition. Our twin cities briefly reconnected in 2019 when the BBC requested that Lady Godiva fly free on our Town Hall flagpole astride her horse, though 25 long years had passed.
Give Me a "C!"

We begin with our storied champions who stand the test of time. Go, Patriots! was the rallying cry at each pep rally and basketball game, meant to revere our historic hometown hero from the 1700s, Nathan Hale. Hale's gutsy 1776 declaration was, "I regret that I have only one life to give for my country." But Lady G's enthralling activism in 1057 was way ahead of its time. Responding to a dare by her husband, she cantered naked on horseback, ending an unfair tax on the citizens of Coventry, luscious locks her only armour. Give Me an "O!"

Recollections summoned fond reminiscences of traveling abroad 50+ years ago. Watching the July 20, 1969 US moon landing perched on the Lord Mayor's chesterfield. Discovering Gooseberry pie, performing at the "Royal Show' and Coventry Cathedral. Anticipating the marvels of a city with 300,000 residents juxtaposed against the 12,000 good people who resided in our quiet farming community.
Give Me a "V!"

Revering the past is a pleasant diversionary exercise for the brain's working memory. And so my postcards to Emilie Lauren Jones were meant to lift us out of recent darkness. A photography excursion around town resulted in custom 5x7 postcard images intended to share tales that identified how we became who we are. The 1825 still-standing one-room schoolhouse, renowned herbalist Adelma Grenier Simmons of Caprilands Herb Farm distinction, world-famous sculptor David Hayes and, of course, Nathan Hale's family homestead.

Give Me an "E!"

I researched our twinning connection for Roze Navab's podcast and learned about the 26 cities across the globe, of which only three are named Coventry; the holly trees of the Wyken Peace Garden chosen to honor those settlements; triangular Godcakes imbued with religious intention for New Year's Eve. And the November 14, 1940 bombing of Coventry Cathedral, a leap year, 366 days instead of 365 destined to align the solar system with civilization's calendar. But as this ominous event proves, those intercalary days are calamitous harbingers. Consider 2020, another such lockdown, when the portentous event now recognized as the global pandemic rode in straddling that angry black steed branded Covid-19. (No offense to the genteel, brave Lady Godiva.)

Give Me an "N!"

I loved linking past and present through the deceivingly simple, disciplined task of sending postcards to the willing, beating heart of an unknown other. Love is at the core of peace and reconciliation, the thing that keeps hope alive. For what is twinning but, much like Lady Godiva, showing up in the fullness of our collective, vulnerable humanity?

Give Me a "TRY!"

EMILIE LAUREN JONES

## Three Ways to Start the Day

*Inspired by the lives of Nathan Hale,*
*Adelma Grenier Simmons and David Hayes*

*i*

September sunshine,
a Sunday morning walk
past rows of scarlet coats,
bayonets accusing a silent sky.
One firm kick is all that's needed
to overthrow the keg,
the open-mouthed noose purses –
we only have one life to lose
and he would lose it again again again…

*ii*

6am tastes of mint tea and chopped basil.
Flowers bloom from her hat,
her cloak swishes
as she passes through the back door.
This ground knew the happy trot of cloven hooves,
later today, another fleet of chattering heels
will arrive with questions and leave with books.
Perhaps, it is possible to grow a better world
with paper and soil and a sapling of excitement.

*iii*

He gazes at the tiny globes of dew,
imagines stretching out the colours
of Earth's reflection
twisting them into the shape of a woman.
Yesterday, he presented a wreath of steel flowers to the sun.
Today, he spots a space
behind that apple tree,
imagines squeezing periwinkles from the sky
and moulding them into aluminium smiles.

**Image: Lorsen Camps – 'Paperweight Globes'**

(photograph from the Charity Shop Found Objects series)

EUROPE
ATLANTIC
ALGERIA
LIBYA
SAHARA
AFRICA
EGYPT
SUDAN
ZAIRE
TANZANIA
BRAZIL
SOUTH AMERICA
OCEAN
INDIAN
LIBYA
EGYPT
IRAQ
SAUDI ARABIA
ATLANTIC
FRENCH WEST AFRICA
OCEAN

I
DRESDEN

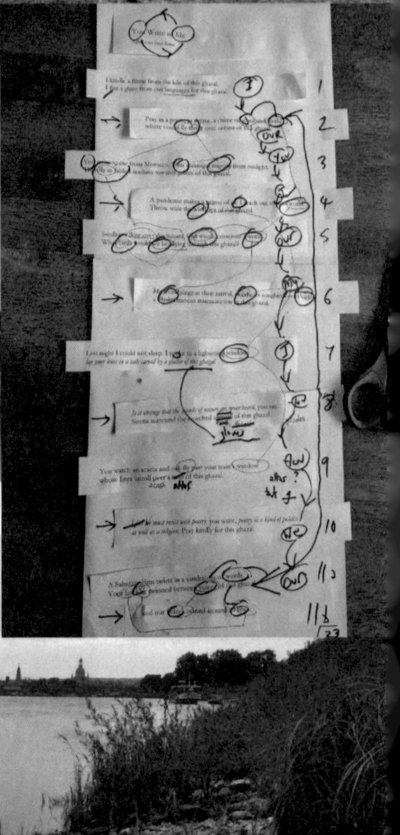
You Write to Me

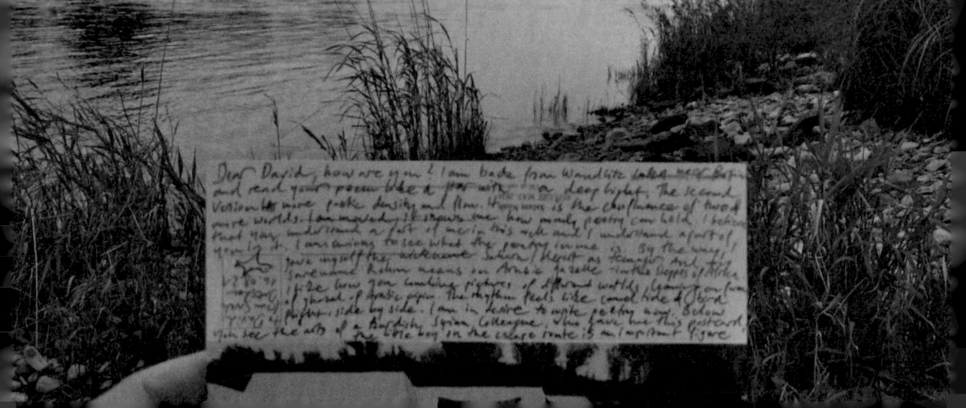
Dear David, how are you?

# DRESDEN

## Germany

*Twinned in 1959*

51°03′00″N 13°44′24″E
657 miles from Coventry

SARAH AMMAJOU REHM

DAVID MORLEY

SARAH AMMAJOU REHM

# menschen stürzen wie tränen

ein lied für euch

´(S)*ome of the greatest Sufi poets of the ghazal were from Afghanistan including Rumi and Ansari.´* *

aus einer E-Mail von David Morley

*„Einige der größten Sufi-Dichter des Ghazal kamen aus Afghanistan, darunter Rumi und Ansari."

meine stimme ist erschüttert, jedes mal außerhalb des krieges
bestrafe ich mich dass sie ihn nicht verhinderte, ich schweige

die pandemie zeigte mir, wer ich bin, wenn mein pass nicht gilt
ich durfte nicht von Europa nach Afrika zu meinem liebsten

ich entkam dem lockdown auf die inseln der Kanaren,
sie gehörten doch Marokko, ich sah stattliche villen von deutschen

als ich endlich die wüste erreichte, war ich eine adlerin, bedroht
und versteckte meine stimme wieder, diesmal in einem regime

deine adleraugen folgten mir, im grünen beflüstertest du ein pferd
ich? erspähte pinienwäldern, haschischfelder, glaubte, höheres zu sehen

wir fuhren an der küste entlang, an der die boote ablegen der illegalen
das mittelmeer versucht uns allen ständig signale zu senden

im Coventry War Memorial Park denkmal, in der kammer des schweigens
lies´ die liste von männern von dort, die in welt- und golfkriegen starben

´The natural world (...) was what I inhabited with all my mind.´, *
  schreibst du
ich weiß, dass auch wir nun unser Zuhause verlieren werden
*„Die Natur (...) war das, was ich mit meinem erfüllten Geist bewohnte. ",
  schreibst du

nahe Fez: der opa meines mannes lächelte, ein schäfer, an französischer Front
über deutsche: umzingelt auf dem hügel, verbissen, benutzten
menschenschilde

England can be so insular that it almost seems ashamed of itself, * sagst du,
und im flugzeug nach Deutschland weiß ich: wir alle sind verstreut
*England kann so abgeschottet sein, dass es sich fast zu schämen scheint

ich wünschte ich fände die brunnen, die uns zum frieden heilen
erschüfe den sandsturm mit worten, in dem menschen sanft in sicherheit
fliegen

zumindest tauchen unsere stimmen auf, als Afghanistan verschwindet
kein trost, nur klarheit: mögen mich die lieder der ungehörten tief
erschüttern und ich

schweigen

## people falling like tears

a song for you

*„(S)ome of the greatest Sufi poets of the ghazal were from Afghanistan including Rumi and Ansari."*
*from an email by David Morley*

my voice is shaken, every time outside of war
I punish myself that she did not prevent him, I am silent

the pandemic showed me who I am when my passport is not valid
I was not allowed to go from Europe to Africa to meet my loved one

I escaped the lockdown to the Canary Islands
by earth they belonged to Morocco, I saw stately villas by Germans

when I finally reached the desert I was an eagle, endangered
and I hid my voice again, this time it was in a regime

your eagle eyes followed me, in the green you whispered to a horse
me? spied pine forests, fields of hashish, believing living higher things

we drove along the coast, where the boats drop off the illegal
the mediterranean tries to send signals to all of us all the time

in Coventry War Memorial Park monument in the Chamber of Silence
read the list of men from there lost life in World and Gulf Wars

'The natural world (...) was what I inhabited with all my mind.', you write
I know we will lose our home now too

near Fez, my husband's grandpa, shepherd, smiled, at French front
over Germans, encircled on a hill, using, grimly, civilians as shields

England can be so insular that it almost seems ashamed of itself, you say,
and on the plane to Germany I know: we are all scattered

I wish I found the wells that heal us to peace,
create in words the sandstorm in which people gently fly to safety

at least our voices appear, when Afghanistan disappears,
no solace, only clarity: may the songs of the unheard shake me deeply
    and I be

silence

**Translated by the poet.**

## Note on 'People falling like tears'

David Morley, my twin city poet, lives in Coventry, where I have never been, and I found out it has a memorial park. I began to think about, what would happen, if at the "Role of the Fallen" in the memorial would be listed not only the men from Coventry, but from all around the world, who died, and everybody, everywhere, and every memorial in the world would list all the dead from all wars to understand what this means. Is this possible?

While I was travelling, David gave me views on his relationship as poet to the nature, the birds, and how he is teaching poetry for example by taking a woman out to see a horse, he is talking to; he sent me a photo of the conversation. He asked me, which birds are living in Dresden, which I had never thought about before.

My home is travel. I live in Dresden, a city which has a sad past in a double sense and is known today from the racist movement, which has used the centre there for years to do stupid demonstrations. But we resist. For example, I am writing together with refugees to tell their stories, and I also support elderly people to tell of their experiences in the DDR.

David and I exchanged about the source of our poetry and about political questions, climate change, migration.

I leaned my poem on the form of David's poem, who studied the ghazal, which began to fascinate me, too; I used it in an open way. It became a song for the people of Afghanistan, since I am touched a lot by the happenings in the days of the writing of the poem.

I found so much in the history of Europe, Africa, in my travels and in David's and mine exchange and our emotions that belongs to Afghanistan, that I saw Afghanistan become the world.

May we listen to the unheard voices.

David Morley, mein Dichter aus der Zwillingsstadt, lebt in Coventry, wo ich noch nie war, und ich habe herausgefunden, dass es dort einen Gedenkpark gibt. Ich begann darüber nachzudenken, was passieren würde, wenn auf der „Rolle der Gefallenen" in der Gedenkstätte nicht nur die Männer aus Coventry aufgeführt würden, sondern aus aller Welt, die gestorben sind, und alle, überall, und an jedem Gedenkort der Welt würden alle Toten aller Kriege aufgeführt, um zu verstehen, was dies bedeutet. Ist dies möglich?

Auf meinen Reisen erzählte mir David von seiner Beziehung als Dichter zur Natur, zu den Vögeln und wie er Poesie lehrt, indem er zum Beispiel eine Frau nach draußen mitnimmt, um ein Pferd zu sehen, mit dem er spricht; er schickte mir ein Foto des Gesprächs. Er fragte mich, welche Vögel in Dresden leben, worüber ich mir noch nie Gedanken gemacht hatte.

Mein Zuhause ist die Reise. Ich lebe in Dresden, einer Stadt, die im doppelten Sinne eine traurige Vergangenheit hat und heute aus der rassistischen Bewegung bekannt ist, die dort seit Jahren das Zentrum für dumme Demonstrationen nutzt. Aber wir wehren uns. Ich schreibe zum Beispiel gemeinsam mit Flüchtlingen ihre Geschichten, und ich unterstütze auch ältere Menschen, ihre Erfahrungen in der DDR zu erzählen.

David und ich tauschten uns über die Quelle unserer Poesie und über politische Fragen, Klimawandel, Migration aus.

Ich lehnte mein Gedicht an die Form von Davids Gedicht an, der das Ghazal studierte, was mich auch zu faszinieren begann; ich habe es offen genutzt. Es wurde ein Lied für das afghanische Volk, da ich sehr berührt bin von den Ereignissen in den Tagen, als das Gedicht geschrieben wurde.

Ich habe in der Geschichte Europas, Afrikas, auf meinen Reisen und in Davids und meinem Austausch und unseren Emotionen so viel gefunden, das zu Afghanistan gehört, dass ich sah, Afghanistan wurde zur Welt.

Mögen wir auf die ungehörten Stimmen hören.

## DAVID MORLEY

# The Mist Net Releases Her Birds

Ghazal for Sarah

*I wished to create a sandstorm with words in which people would gently fly to safety*

– from a postcard by Sarah Rehm

You open a window to the morning mist of this ghazal.
I release songbirds from the mist net of this ghazal.

You write to me from Morocco. Your messages migrate from sunlight.
They fly in fabled feathers towards gables of this ghazal.

A pandemic makes prisoners of us. I reach out to you
across Spain and the Bay of Biscay from this ghazal.

Swifts swoop over the Sahara. Our words crisscross a world.
What birds would we be, flowing through this ghazal?

Morning sings with their landfall, overhears swallows over oases,
the Mediterranean murmurating in this ghazal.

You watch an acacia and oak fly past your train's window.
Their leaf-tips unfurl in the forest of this ghazal.

'It is strange that the sounds of nature are never heard', you say.
Silence surrounds the singing glades of this ghazal.

'We resist through poetry', you write, 'poems are a kind
of politics as well as religion'. Pray kindly for this ghazal.

A Saharan *djinn* twists in a sirocco of words.
Your lines spin twinned between voices of this ghazal

and our voices twine around its lines.
Open the mist net. Throw wide the windows of this ghazal.

## Note on 'The Mist Net Releases Her Birds'

The poet Sarah Rehm lives in one of Coventry's twin cities, Dresden. However, when we first wrote to each other, Sarah was travelling in Morocco and her postcards were full of vibrant and vivid descriptions. I was emerging from the Covid-19 lockdown in England and was transported by her written accounts of travel, freedom, and sunlight. They inspired the images of places, birds, and migration. The Arabic poetic form, the ghazal, seemed natural for the poem. I also wove in some phrases from Sarah's postcards.

It is common in ghazals for the poet's name to be featured like a flourished signature towards the end of the poem. Instead, I chose to offer Sarah's name because of the presence of her words and the image of the Sahara. I sent the poem to Sarah. The epigraph is a phrase from her beautiful response.

Sarah and I live and write in twin cities. This ghazal is a twin form in its use of couplets; the speaking in turn of two voices; and because we both had a hand and voice in making this poem. Thank you.

Your lines spin twinned between voices of this ghazal

and our voices twine around its lines.

**Image: Andy Farr – 'Regeneration'**

"MISTY" THE SOUND OF
graz
Der Text
als Landschaft
GRAZ. DIE KULTURHAUPTSTADT

# GRAZ

## Austria

*Twinned in 1957*

47°04′15″N 15°26′19″E
839 miles from Coventry

PETRA GANGLBAUER

PETER RAYNARD

PETRA GANGLBAUER

# From St. Albans to Graz

(With Peter Raynard)

*Summer 2021*

Words and pictures
Travelling from here to there –
Filled with history and phantasy.
That is to say: POETRY.

Was amazing
Was colourful
Was warm-hearted
This dialogue from me to you –
From you to me –

Was not a dream.

The picture-postcards sailed
Over Summer-Fields, the Sea
And all the urban squares.
They interrupted the enclosing
Global atmosphere
Stamp by stamp.

And finally I got a shining idea
From St. Albans and
Keep it in my memory:
My mother tongue.

PETER RAYNARD

## Poem for Petra

Your cards of Graz were nightingales flying
through a squall. Messages of an elsewhere
with green shoots that emblem your city.
The tree-clad fortress of ancient Schlossberg

its funicular ticking up to a towering clock.
I learned of your city's lustre, how the face
of a place is a steady companion against
the tides of the world's shifting shores

ready when we're able to swim once more.
Your cards from Graz were a visit to its arts,
the stickleback museum Kunsthaus, Murinsel
that floats like a sapphire on the River Mur.

Your cards from Graz made me think
of old friends how our links are now distilled
by isolation into WhatsApp lines, emojis,
Dad jokes, but happy that our Sky Blue boys

continue to shine. Your card from Graz
in the Ausgarten snow when you were young
took me back to my short trouser days
playing with friends down the fields at the end

of my road, jumping brooks, running like rabbits
away from horses. My cards of Coventry told
of a city that wears its history well. A Phoenix
ever-rising from an age-old blaze of social change

a refuge for those fleeing wars they never made.
Sent to Coventry is no longer an enemy's gaol.
My cards of Coventry told you 'County' Coundon
was my home, with Irish friends whose fathers

helped re-build the city time and again. When
I next see my Coventry, I will think of Graz
its images as memories of a newfound friend.

**Image: Ayesha Jones – 'Meritah'**

南 Jinan / Tsinan

# JINAN

济南市

China

*Twinned in 1983*

36°40′13″N 117°01′15″E
5,258 miles from Coventry

SUN LEI

ANTONY OWEN

## SUN LEI

# 济南或者考文垂

给安东尼

这是不安的一年，
一切都在双重甚至多重的压力下
成为流水。
灾难流过来，人们毫无察觉，
尽管它更立体，有多面性的反光。

济南或者考文垂
屠城或被轰炸，现在
历史用遗迹理解和平，
我们用诗。

我们用音乐和绘画，
我们是暗的
我们相互坐的很远，挨得很近，
我们挤在旷野上
我们互为篝火
我们是暗的
我们也是火

济南或者考文垂
越明亮的天空越虚无
在隔离中
我们虚脱。我们不能一直虚脱，
一直站在彼此的遥远里
像一个无所事事的孩子，
哭着长大。

2021年8月16日

# Jinan or Coventry

*To Antony*

This is an unpeaceful year,
Everything is under double or even multiple pressures
Becoming flowing water.
Disaster has followed, people are unaware of it,
Although it is more three-dimensional, it has multi-faceted reflections.

Jinan or Coventry
Massacred or bombed, Now
History understands peace with ruins,
We use poetry.

We use music and painting,
We are dark
We sit very far, but close to each other,
We are huddling in the wilderness
We are each other's bonfire
We are dark
We are also fire

Jinan or Coventry
The brighter the sky, the more unreal
In isolation
We collapse. We cannot collapse all the time,
Always standing far away from each other
Like a child who has nothing to do,
Grown up crying.

*August 16, 2021*

**Translated by the poet.**

# 雪

给 Antony

雪，下在身上，火炉边
雪不化，读书的手上，有一座俄国的山
白雪覆盖山顶，记忆埋葬死亡

雪人有黑色的面孔，
雪的白，以光的力量
照向黑人、黄种人、亚洲人
照着黑色的土地，照着喉咙
以及，喉咙中呛人的
烟尘。

雪落在石头上，石头的柔软
在空中延展，像滕蔓，它要抓住远方，
它以雪的名义，抓住你我的
温暖

抓住，那些济南或者考文垂的工厂里
不断响起的机器的轰鸣声。

# Snow

*To Antony*

Snow, falling on the body, by the fire
The snow does not melt. There is a Russian mountain in the
    hand of reading
Snow covers the mountain, memory buries death.

The snowman has a black face,
Snow white, with the power of light
Black, yellow, Asian
Shining on the black land, shining on the throat
And choking in the throat
Soot.

The snow fell on the stone, and the stone was soft
Stretching in the air, like a vine, it wants to catch the distance,
It catches warmth of you and me
I n the name of snow

Hold on, those factories in Jinan or Coventry
The constant roar of the machine.

**Translated by the poet.**

## ANTONY OWEN

# Flying in Jinan

*(written in syllabic structure of a haiku)*

In the rush hour smog
on Jinan's floating bridges
meet me on the air.

In the typhoon eye
meet me there before we lift
let us rain upwards.

These golden temples –
temporary as our sun
spinning not flying.

Read me a poem.
I shall close my eyes and fly
on wings of old books.

I will read you Hughes,
his crow shall remind us both
the crueller natures of man.

At Red Leaves Canyon
let's look in ancient rivers
leaving our wrinkles

In Coventry
a phoenix once flew
like you and I friend.

# Kin

I picture our human ancestors
catching the whispers of Ji and Sherbourne.
Beneath Coventry's skin our river weaves her sky-blue veins
her pulse strongest in Spon End where worlds in tenements meet.

So, my distant friend, each river sheds her parchment onto land.
What secrets would the restless Ji spill from her mouth?
Crystalline perhaps? Or your eyes precious stones?
feeding white hair from waterfalls of Mount Tai.

I think of dusk over your moat of mountains.
Nightfall is an empress dragging her dynasties' robe,
red for statues, gold for rebirth to wax the rivers skin by morn.
To bejewel the abdomens of dragonfly and tattoo the moth in abandon.

So, my distant friend, my Saxon city is Jinan's unlikely twin.
Both are weavers with wet threads splitting bedrock.
Read about our mountains of November fourteenth,
they were lowly emperors of a different dragon.

I picture our human ancestors
waiting at the shore for us on the day we cross over.
I split a mandarin into two pieces and give you one half,
we listen to Confucius preaching how in heaven we feed one another.

*2021.8.23*

Image: Mandip Singh Seehra – 'Bridge to the colourful world'

FRIENDS
JAMAICA
Rafting on the Martha Brae River
JAMA

# KINGSTON
## Jamaica

*Twinned in 1962*

17°58′17″N 76°47′35″W
4,623 miles from Coventry

TANYA SHIRLEY

ROMALYN ANTE

TANYA SHIRLEY

## Poets Don't Tell You Everything

On a postcard with a bridge and bright yellow umbrella
you tell me you were born in a village called Riverside.
We write these notes as a bridge from Coventry to Kingston.
I want to be a flashlight fish in the water beneath us,
my reflective strip shimmering like a street dancer
not dodging soda bottles, construction site glass, bread bags
but we are living in the season of decay, twinned
because out of slavery, out of the labour shortage,
out of the war, my people found themselves in Coventry.
What about reparations? Instead, two poets make worlds
out of words, twining our desire for that which washes
away, an undercurrent of all we cannot say
on this page so small, so square, so public.
I am afraid my elderly in-laws will die while
we sort out quarantines, vaccines, visas, red lists.
You write about family in the Philippines and I fall
into the sinkhole of          *This is not my home.*
    *Is this home?*          *Are you home?*
I tell you Kingston is hot and the beaches far
on the back of a touristy postcard which will not
reach you before the end of summer, our cursive
caught in the slime of an Atlantic crossing as if
our existence is liminal. No wonder we praise water,
waiting to wash ashore with scales so luminous
those on the bridge, even the bright yellow umbrella
will finally wonder how many more of us are down there
dying.

ROMALYN ANTE

# The River Tells me its Secrets

A child's cry is born out of water.
The tortoise and the moon-
eating dragon, all born out of water.

Everything begins in this river.
Everything is endured by this river.
A poet's larynx is a stream

where the gods flung
their unvarnished stars.
The waters bear the names

of my grandmothers, unnames the men
who built stone huts along its banks.
At dinadala ng agos mga alaala.

Duon, sa may bato –
kung saan ikaw at ako
ay tumalon, papihit na parang trumpo.

Where does my river end and begin –
the mouth of a cave, at the tip
of a borrowed tongue? Last night,

I walked around Coventry, knowing
the Sherbourne flows beneath
this town – no matter how much

the body gets tired,
the stream pushes through the dark.
Soon, it will join the Sowe,

the Avon. The river reminds me
of its secrets. Syllables
of yellow pebbles

shift towards light.

**Image: Paramjit Sehmi – 'Golden'**

# VOLGOGRAD

## Волгоград

## Russia

*Twinned in 1944*

**48°42′31″N 44°30′53″E**
**3,370 miles from Coventry**

OLGA IGUMNOVA LAWSON

AMANDA DALTON

## OLGA IGUMNOVA LAWSON

Познавшие все тяготы войны,
Народы мира смотрят с ожиданьем:
Неужто ль снова силы злые тьмы,
Завеют ветры скорби и отчаянья?

We do remember horror things of war,
We, people of the world, and we are waiting.
Are there new and Evil Dawns
And new winds of new tragedies approaching?

Но нет, встают во весь рост города,
Как Фениксы восставшие из пепла.
И говорят любви и счастью – да,
Шлют пожеланья света, мира всем нам.

And look – the cities stand together now
Like Phoenixes are rising from the ashes.
They stand for light, for peace, for love
And sending everyone support and healthy wishes.

Мы помним тех, живя в руинах кто,
Способен был другим прийти на помощь.
В Объединении наций, городов –
Вот в это мирной жизни есть вся мощь.

We do remember those, lived in ruins,
Were ready to give help to other victims.
Uniting efforts, cities, nations –
That is the might of peaceful foundation.

AMANDA DALTON

## Postcards to Olga

I'm reading about a tablecloth
stitched with hundreds of signatures
and sent across a devastated world

of women who never touched,
never met, but wrote
with the indelible ink of thread.

***

If I google-map a line that runs
from Coventry to Volgograd
crossing water, borders, time zones,

door-to-door it says from my old house
to Nickolay Otrada Street
will take a day and nineteen hours.

***

Let's imagine a table that spans
over two thousand miles,
and a cotton cloth spread over it

and all the bombed-out women
sitting, sharing soup, embroidering
their words of solidarity and hope.

***

Here these days it sometimes seems
we've turned our backs on everything.
Do strangers hug in Volgograd?

Bump elbows? Feet?
Do your arms sometimes reach out
as mine do, meeting air and light?

Let's write.

**Poet's Note:** Volgograd (formerly Stalingrad) was almost completely destroyed in a devastating German onslaught and ensuing battle during WW2. The people of Coventry, having experienced the horror of the Coventry Blitz a few years earlier, sent supplies to the citizens of Stalingrad and women signed their names, which were then embroidered onto a tablecloth and sent with messages of solidarity and hope. Coventry and Volgograd (re-named in 1961) became the first cities to Twin – now a global movement.

**Image: Frances Yeung – 'United Hands'**

Warszawa
PAŁAC KULTURY
I NAUKI

MERMAID OF WA

SAVIOUR SQUARE

# WARSAW

**Warszawa**

**Poland**

*Twinned in 1957*

52°14′N 21°1′E
947 miles from Coventry

MARCIN NIEWIROWICZ

ANDREA MBARUSHIMANA

Image: postcards designed and illustrated
by the poet, Marcin Niewirowicz.

MARCIN NIEWIROWICZ

## raport z innego miasta

chciałbym żeby widok się zmienił a trawa
była bardziej zielona bo jeśli jest płot zawsze
będzie jakaś strona i trawa jest inna i inne są
słowa po drugiej stronie tęczy

– dawno już spalona – rac nie żałuj
i pochodni nie żałuj róż nie żałuj lasów
będzie więcej burz i więcej hałasu proszę
zmilcz że trawa tak samo zielona

i widok ten sam lecz wciąż mamy problemy
z koła kwadraturą i słowa doborem sianiem
wiatru i obroną pola przedstaw się ładnie
– o ironio –

milcz gdy trzmiel się w trawie schowa tu
jest moja ulica tu jest rzeka i pałac a to moja
głowa pochylona w pozie pokutnej będę
pokutować – taka jest umowa

postaw się postaw na przestrzeni języka tu
jest twoje miejsce tu płot a tu obręcz stalowa
moja część będzie martwa nigdy nie
skończona ledwie w formie przypisu

do zdarzeń nad którymi przejdziemy do
porządku bo tak wygodnie się mieszka
i całkiem bezpiecznie ale tylko jeśli ucichnę
tylko jeśli się schowam nawet jeśli krzyknę –

nikt nikt mnie nie obroni i nikt zawoła

# report from another city

I wish the view changed and the grass was greener
for if there is a fence there is always some side and
the grass is different and the words are different on
the other side of the rainbow

– burned long ago – don't be upset about flares
and torches don't be upset about roses about forests
more storms'll come and more noise please
keep mum about the grass being the same green

and the view is the same but we still have problems
with squaring the circle and choosing the words
sowing the wind and defending the field introduce
yourself nicely – what irony –

don't squeal when a bumblebee hides in the grass
here is my street here is the river and the palace and
this is my head bowed in repentance I'll repent –
that's the deal

put yourself within the space of language here
is your place here is the fence and here is the frame of
steel my part will be dead never finished barely in
a form of a footnote

to the events that we'll gloss over because
it's so comfortable to live and quite safe but only if
I keep quiet only if I conceal myself and even if
I shout –

no one to defend me and no one to call out

**Translated by the poet.**

ANDREA MBARUSHIMANA

# The Totems of Coventry and Warsaw Imagine Meeting

*It would be good,* thinks Elephant
*to have a cup of tea with Mermaid*
*to see her sat here, shedding scales like sequins at a disco.*

Elephant walks through town, imagines seeing Mermaid there
sketching a postcard of the council house – squid ink and rainbows
But Mermaid might be listening for her mother tongue
missing the lap of waves, the burping of fishes
through Elephant's cacophony of purchases and arguments
the vortex of the ring-road?

*We just wanted a cup of tea together,* Elephant thinks
Why do all these anxieties disturb our dreams?

Elsewhere Mermaid is trying to translate her thoughts
into a language Elephant can understand:
The sonic boom of distant thunderstorms
*Will Elephant ever know,* she asks
*my hearts longing for water?*

Elephant misses the old swimming baths
turns on a tap
nothing comes out but hand-gel.

## POET BIOGRAPHIES

**Romalyn Ante** is a Filipino-born, Wolverhampton-based poet, editor, and essayist. She is co-founding editor of *harana poetry*, an online magazine for poets writing in English as a second or parallel language. Her debut collection is *Antiemetic for Homesickness* (Chatto & Windus). Her honours include the Poetry London Clore Prize, Manchester Poetry Prize, Society of Authors Foundation Award, and Creative Future Literary Award. Her work has been featured in BBC World News, World Literature Today, BBC Radio 4, *Harper's Bazaar, Vogue* UK, Southbank Centre, *Poetry Review*, amongst others.

**Raef Boylan** has been featured at spoken word gigs and festivals around the Midlands. In 2019, he was selected to represent Coventry poets overseas in Cork, Ireland. His writing, recently commissioned by Theatre Absolute and BBC Radio, has appeared in various publications. Raef also organises monthly poetry event 'Fire & Dust' and is chief editor of award-winning magazine *Here Comes Everyone.*

**Amanda Dalton** is a poet and playwright from Coventry, now living in West Yorkshire. *How To Disappear* and *Stray* are published by Bloodaxe and she is currently completing a pamphlet and a third full-length collection. She writes extensively for BBC Radio 4 and 3. Work for theatre includes commissions with Manchester's Royal Exchange and Sheffield Theatres. She has worked as a Deputy Headteacher, Arvon Centre Director and as a senior creative leader in theatre. Amanda is an RLF Fellow and visiting lecturer in the Writing School at Manchester Metropolitan University. Her website is amandadalton.co.uk

**Olga Dermott Bond's** first pamphlet *apple, fallen* was published by Against the Grain Press in 2020, and her second collection *A Sky full of strange specimens* is published by Nine Pens Press. She has won a number of poetry competitions including the BBC Proms poetry competition. Originally from Northern Ireland, she lives in Warwickshire. She is a teacher and has two daughters.

**Petra Ganglbauer** was born in Graz, and has been living and working in Vienna and Burgenland, and with different projects in Italy, Germany, Rumania and Austria. Many travels. Publications of Lyrics, Prose and Essay. Audio Pieces. Intermedial Project-Conceptions. Literary Workshops. ganglbauer.mur.at

**Aysar Ghassan** loves the possibilities contained in unwritten poems and the adventures that writing allows him to go on. His work has been published in journals like *Magma, The Interpreter's House, Under The Radar* and *Strix.* He has participated in the Coventry-Cork twin cities exchange, headlined The Kenilworth Arts Festival and is currently a Dynamo mentee with Nine Arches Press.

**Olga Igumnova** has experienced life in the USSR, modern Russia and the European Union. She learnt about Coventry at the age of 8 in English lessons at school in Volgograd and has been involved in Volgograd and Coventry projects since, the latest project is:
https://coventry2021.co.uk/get-involved/coventry-x-volgograd-digital-tablecloth-call-out/

**Emilie Lauren Jones** has previously been published in *HCE* Magazine and I am not a silent poet. She is due to be published in upcoming anthologies with Half Moon Books, Beautiful Dragons Collaborations and One World Publications. Commissioned by the UK City of Culture project 'Humans of Cov', she is also part of the current Nine Arches Press Dynamo Scheme.

Translator **Dušica Karaić** studies in two faculties at the University of Belgrade. While in high school, she attended national competitions in literature called "Književna olimpijada", winning 1st place in 2019. Since June 2020 she has been working as a coordinator for the Young Writers Association of Serbia. She worked alongside the president of the Association to recreate the magazine *Zmaj*. Her main passion is writing prose and poetry. Two short stories are soon to be published in a creative writing anthology called *Reč po reč.*

**Victoria Kennefick's** first collection, *Eat or We Both Starve,* was published by Carcanet Press in March 2021. Her pamphlet, *White Whale* (Southword Editions, 2015), won the Munster Literature Centre Fool for Poetry Chapbook Competition and the Saboteur Award for Best Poetry Pamphlet. She is a recipient of a Next Generation Artist Award from the Arts Council of Ireland.

**Sun Lei's** works were translated to English, French, and Spanish, German, Korean. He has been shown his works at Weiming Poetry Festival of Peking University, North Europe Art Festival, USA Boston International Poetry Festival, The China Millennium Monument International Poetry Festival, Qinghai International Poetry Festival, East Asia International Poetry Festival, and South Africa International Poetry Festival. He is a poet, professor and painter based in Jinan, China.

**Andrea Mbarushimana:** Coventry born writer, artist and community connnector, Andrea has recently completed poetry commissions for Theatre Absolute's *Humanistan* project and the Digi Poems project for the BBC Contains Strong Language Festival. *Fatbergs,* her third poetry pamphlet was recently launched by Knives Forks and Spoons Press. You can find all her other publications and projects at andrea.mbarushimana.com.

**Susan MacNeil** grew up in rural Coventry, Connecticut, a wooded environment that invoked a sense of freedom to roam. This liberty birthed a love of words that dwelled restlessly in her pocket, waiting to labor on paper and pen. And so she embraces twinning in uninhibited broad brush strokes, bonding with unknown others from around the globe who dare to show up in the fullness of our collective, vulnerable humanity.

**David Morley** was trained as a freshwater ecologist. He won the Ted Hughes Award for *The Invisible Gift: Selected Poems.* His latest book *FURY* was a Poetry Book Society Choice and shortlisted for the Forward Prize for Best Collection. David is a Fellow of The Royal Society of Literature and teaches at Warwick University.

**#narrandoBo,** founded in 2018, is an artistic collective dedicated to Bologna, telling stories of the city with the collaboration of artists from the region. The project has three artistic directors: **Leonardo Bianconi** author and actor; **Giulia Quadrelli** author and actress; **Leo Merati** author, actor, videomaker. Bologna is celebrated through poetry, standup, music, theatre, video, comics, radio drama and more.

**Marcin Niewirowicz** is a poet, photographer and librarian at the National Library of Poland. He was twice shortlisted for a major Polish poetry award, the Jacek Bierezin Prize (2014, 2016), and received the Artur Fryz Prize commendation (2018). His poems were featured in many prestigious literary magazines in Poland. His two volumes of poetry are: *Dociekania strefy* (Nisza, 2017) and *Wszystkie ptaszki, które miałem w garści* (Nisza, 2020).

**Antony Owen** is a writer from Coventry and the author of six poetry collections since 2009. His latest collection is *Cov Kids* (Knives Forks and Spoons Press). His previous collection, *The Nagasaki Elder* was shortlisted for the coveted Ted Hughes Award and he is one of the leading writers of war and peace poetry active in 21st century poetry. His work is taught at regular poetry workshops in Hiroshima and also appears in a national UK peace education resource by CND Peace Education.

**Peter Raynard** is a writer and editor of Proletarian Poetry: poems of working class lives. He has been widely published and his debut collection *Precarious* was published by Smokestack Books in April 2018. His poetic coupling of the Communist Manifesto was published by Culture Matters in May, 2018.

**Sarah Rehm** was born in Dachau and lives in Dresden. She writes poetry and prose and is the founder of writing workshops 'Strong Quills' and the intercultural project, 'TellYourTruth'. She is a trained writing therapist, refugee helper, and mentors women in academia and research. She has published poetry and prose in literary magazines such as *die Horen* and *EDIT*, has received several scholarships, and has participated in the renowned 'Klagenfurt literature course'.

**Tanya Shirley** has published two poetry collections with Peepal Tree Press in the UK: *She Who Sleeps With Bones* and *The Merchant of Feathers.* Her work has been featured on BBC World Service, BBC Front Row, Scottish Poetry Library, www.poetryarchive.org and translated into Spanish and Polish. Shirley is a lecturer in the Department of Literatures in English at The University of the West Indies, Mona Campus. She is the recipient of a Silver Musgrave Medal from the Institute of Jamaica for her outstanding contribution in the field of Literature. She is also a proud Cave Canem Fellow.

**Mihajlo Zilovic** is a young Serbian writer of poetry and prose. He has published Monographs of Serbian Writers and is the president of The Young Writers Association of Serbia. Mihajlo is a student of two faculties at The University of Belgrade. He is the editor-in-chief of the literary magazine *Zmaj*. He has won awards in the field of literature and art and his poems have been in many publications and daily newspapers. His first book of poems is soon to be published.

## ARTIST BIOGRAPHIES

**Lorsen Camps** is a Coventry-based artist revealing the beauty he sees in disregarded materials. His work has featured in selected shows such as the Royal Academy Summer Exhibition and won the Leamington Open in 2019. He has organised a number of solo and group exhibitions including partnering with The Mead Gallery and the Herbert Art Gallery & Museum. www.lorsencamps.com.

**Mary Courtney:** an artist and poet born and based in Coventry. She has a love of the elephants, the beasts and the mermaids on the buildings of the city - the ridiculous, absurd, the underlooked and overlooked. Right now she is making a big, beautiful "Bling-Road" from bling and stories.www.marycourtneycoventry.com.

**Andy Farr** is an award-winning artist with a strong interest in mental health and well-being. He is currently working on a series of portraits of Coventry's unsung residents, these will be exhibited as part of City of Culture 2021. Previously he has worked with the Institute of Mental Health to tell the stories of people who are recovering from Post-Traumatic Stress. https://www.andyfarr.com

**Gayatri Pasricha** is a UK based graphic designer with a background in philosophy and economics. She strives to combine visual design with her cerebral pursuits. Her designs are playful, but not frivolous; are researched but not complicated; they are subtle but not obscure. You can take a look at her work here: https://guy3.myportfolio.com

**Ayesha Jones** is a dual heritage, neurodiverse, visual artist. She uses photography and film to interrogate social structures and belief systems, through personal narratives. Her autobiographical project, which explores disability, female sexuality and family lineage, was one of 30 projects to receive an international award from Magnum Photos. Ayesha has recently received an award from Unlimited for her latest project, 'Motherland'.
www.ayeshajones.co.uk

**Gurdip Junjuha** is an expressive abstract artist, using art to release emotion and deal with anxiety and depression. She uses art to express how she feels and as therapy. Gurdip has been creating art for the last 30 years. She paints in acrylics and uses vibrant colours to express her emotions using music as an inspiration.

**Adele Mary Reed** was born 1988 in Warwickshire, UK, and is now based in Coventry. She has been experimenting with diaristic images and words from a young age. She carefully collects observations of the places she finds herself in, playfully highlighting the beauty of day-to-day life. She is interested in analogue methodology, walking, plant-life, topographical themes and representations of motherhood. http://www.adelemreed.co.uk.

**Mandip Singh Seehra:** As a photographer I aim to capture the world around me, I have photographed my home city and its communities for a number of years. I enjoy exploring different methodologies in art and photography, experimenting with light and techniques. I have worked with many different artists and people to create images for exhibitions, personal reflection and capturing portraits of Coventry residents. Facebook: Mandip Singh Seehra Photography

**Paramjit Sehmi** was born and raised in Coventry where she developed a natural inclination for art from a young age. She completed her BA and MA degrees in History of Art from the University of Birmingham which contextualised her understanding of art. Paramjit currently works as an Archivist and Visual Artist, exploring her practice through colourful drawings, paintings, and textiles. Website: https://outsidein.org.uk/galleries/paramjit-sehmi/

**Frances Yeung** is a multidisciplinary artist, her works ranging from installations, animations to immersive storytelling, exploring themes related to race and feminist identity. She likes to shine spotlights on marginalised communities, raise awareness of social issues and hope to make real-world changes through her artwork. To see more of her work, visit: yikki.co.uk

## THANKS AND ACKNOWLEDGEMENTS

Thanks are due to all the poets, translators and artists who were part of this project:

Romalyn Ante, Raef Boylan, Amanda Dalton, Olga Dermott-Bond, Petra Ganglbauer, Aysar Ghassan, Olga Igumnova, Emilie Lauren Jones, Dušica Karaić, Victoria Kennefick, Sun Lei, Andrea Mbarushimana, Susan MacNeil, David Morley, #narrandoBo collective: Leonardo Bianconi, Giulia Quadrelli and Leo Merati, Marcin Niewirowicz, Antony Owen, Peter Raynard, Sarah Rehm, Tanya Shirley, Mihajlo Žilović, Allison Grimaldi Donahue, Lorsen Camps, Mary Courtney, Andy Farr, Gayatri Pasricha, Ayesha Jones , Gurdip Junjuha, Adele Mary Reed, Mandip Singh Seehra, Paramjit Sehmi and Frances Yeung.

Also, our thanks to the following people who helped make this project possible by suggest-ing names, connecting poets and translators and supporting us: Neil Astley at Bloodaxe Books, Hannah Bannister at Peepal Tree, Matt Beavers at the British Council, Anna Blaziak, Linda Hirons from Coventry Association for International Friendship (CAIF), Roze Navab, Silvia Sassu and Jennifer Wong. Thanks are due also to Mindy Chillery and Coventry Arstpace, who assisted in the call for artists for the postcards and helped select the ten artworks, and to Mark Cook of Photo Archive Miners who assisted in scanning artworks.

Thanks to colleagues Angela Hicken, Jonathan Davidson and especial thanks to Mollie Davidson, of Creative Lives, for all her research and work in compiling the lists of poets in twin cities and putting us all in touch.

Much gratitude to our project partners as part of BBC Contains Strong Language Festival: Coventry City of Culture Trust, BBC Arts, Writing West Midlands, Creative Lives, the British Council. We gratefully acknowledge funding from Arts Council England and Jerwood Arts.

## ABOUT BBC CONTAINS STRONG LANGAUGE 2021

BBC Contains Strong Language is the BBC's flagship poetry and spoken word festival. Now in its fifth year, the four-day festival is taking place in Coventry, as it celebrates being UK City of Culture 2021 and will broadcast live across BBC Radio and online. It was created by the BBC for Hull City of Culture in 2017, and has taken place annually since then, touring to Cumbria in 2020 before arriving in Coventry for 2021.

BBC Contains Strong Language 2021 is a partnership between the BBC, Coventry City of Culture Trust, Writing West Midlands and Nine Arches Press, and is supported by Arts Council England, the British Council, Creative Lives and Jerwood Arts.

BBC CONTAINS STRONG LANGUAGE

WRITING WEST MIDLANDS

Nine Arches Press

COMMISSIONED BY COVENTRY UK CITY OF CULTURE 2021

Supported using public funding by ARTS COUNCIL ENGLAND

JERWOOD ARTS

BRITISH COUNCIL

Creative Lives